I0487219

Organize Your Home Office!

Over 200 tips to make the most of your space and time

Organize Your Home Office!
Over 200 Tips to Make the Most of Your Space and
Time

Cheryl R. Carter

International Standard Book Number: 9781442101357

Library of Congress Number:00-193357

© Copyright February 2001, Cheryl R. Carter

All rights reserved. No portion of this book may be used
without the written permission of the publisher with
the exception of brief excerpts in magazine articles,
reviews, etc.

Jehonadah Communications
Uniondale, New York 11553-0712

Website www.momtime.net
Email-info@momtime.net

Quantity discounts available.

Organize Your Home Office!

Over 200 tips to make the most of your space and time

Cheryl R. Carter

Jehonadah Communications

Long Island, New York 11553-0712

Dedicated to my mother, Margie
and
My Mother-in-the-Lord, Mina

Two of the best home workers I know!

Acknowledgements

Thanks C.P., I 'm glad you never tire of hearing thank you , as I never tire of saying it.

Thanks to my Three J.'s for enduring the "boring" work while I did something "exciting".

Table of Contents

Section Nine
Frequently Asked Question

Appendix A-Office Supplies

Appendix B-Work at Home Web Sites

Appendix C-Resources

Appendix D-Time Chart

Appendix E-Goal Sheet

Appendix F Organizing Products

Effectiveness demands order!

Section One

Mail System

Mail System

Every home business needs a mail system. Mail should be opened in the same spot everyday. Locate your mail system accordingly. Do not take your mail out of the mailbox until you are ready to file it.

Make a decision on each piece of mail immediately. Then take action on items right away. You should handle correspondence once. Read material that can be read in three minutes or less. Toss junk mail directly into trash. File other materials accordingly.

Get the following multi-colored expandable folders. (Suggested colors white, blue, yellow, red, orange, and green). Use the following folders:

Folder One-White- To Do!

Place items in this folder you need to act on right away. Only place items in this folder you are going to act on within a few days. For example, you may place a magazine you are going to subscribe to, or an invoice you need to dispute. This folder should never be bulky because these items will become part of your daily "to-do" list.

Folder Two- Red-Finances

Place bills in this folder. Also, put a small calendar in this folder. Mark down the date the bill is due and the amount owed. Also mark the bill envelope itself with the same information. It will give you a broad understanding of your business financial position. Note this is not your full fiscal file rather it is your financial correspondence file.

Folder Three-Yellow-Pending

Place items in this folder which are pending, or "on-hold". This will hold the business material that you do not need to take action on right away but information you will need in the future. For example, you may want to order stationary from a mailing you receive. However, you have not yet deleted your stationary supply therefore you cannot act on it immediately. Therefore it will be placed right in this folder until you are ready for it.

Folder Four-Green-To Read

Place items in this folder that will take you longer than three minutes to read. This includes magazines, trade journals and newsletters. This folder should be rather sturdy as you will take it with you whenever there is a possibility you have to wait (i.e. dentist, grocery line, kids soccer practice, etc.)

Folder Four – Blue-To File

Place items in this folder which need to be filed away. Schedule regular times of filing these mail items and other items in your filing cabinet. Receipts, insurance records, etc would go in this folder. When you file weekly these papers should be filed with your other office files.

Folder Five-Orange-To Refer to

Place items in this folder to refer to your business partner, secretary, accountant, lawyer or employee.

Section Two

Files

Files

Every business needs a good filing system. These ideas may help as you devise your filing system. Your files should be easily accessible. Files you seldom refer to should be in your inactive files and may be placed in a storage box or file box..

Inactive/ Active Files

Existing files should be categorized as "active" and "inactive" files. If your files are bulging with outdated information, most likely the majority of your files are inactive files. Inactive files have information you no longer refer to, yet the information cannot thrown away just yet. These files clutter your file cabinet and waste your precious time.

Your filing cabinet should contain files you currently refer to regularly. Remove inactive files and place them in a water proof file box or plastic storage container. Old tax records generally should be placed in the inactive file box.

Categorize your files

Write out your filing categories on paper. Depending on your business your categories may be varied. All files should have a financial section with tax and fiscal information. You may get a copy of Schedule C, for Small Business from the Internal Revenue Service, (IRS) and make your tax files from these categories.

You may simply alphabetize your files into different subjects. This is generally the preferred home office filing. Brochures are filed under letter "B"

Invoices are filed under letter "I". It is very simple to retrieve information with the alphabet plan..

Most home office professionals prefer to use a combination of both. It is helpful to choose categories and then alphabetize within those categories. You may color-code your categories and then alphabetize sub-categories. The type of business you have will determine your categories.

Categories might include: Finances. Project Management, Marketing , Special Projects. Within these categories you would then make sub-categories. For example, look at the way Finances is sub-categorized..

Finances
Sub-categories-
Bills,
Invoices,
Credit card receipts
Accounts receivable

Whichever method you decide to use. You will need to type up a master file sheet to keep a copy on your desk. Or you can insert the sheet in the first file folder in your file cabinet. The sheet will help you easily locate files. Likewise, when you update files or add files you will know where to place the new file.

In addition to filing papers regularly, you will need to purge your file system regularly. This can be done rather systematically. When you go to place a document in a file folder, remove out-dated and unnecessary information.

When you place new documents in your filing cabinet, mark the date the document can be discarded. This way when you go to file new documents you can quickly check which papers are to be removed from the files.

Tickler/ Appointment Files

A tickler file may be necessary if you have appointments that need to be acted on by a certain date. Mark twelve manila folders with the months of the year. Label thirty-one folders with the numbers 1-31, one for each day of the month. Place the current month's folder followed by the numbered folders first in your filing cabinet.

You should then have a folder for each month of the year and folders with the numerals 1-31. This will help you to track information regarding dates.

If you have an appointment October 17th to visit a client, you may put the directions to the clients' house in the number 17-manila folder. If in addition you were scheduled to see another client on November 4th, you would put those directions in the November folder, which would be located behind the numbered manila folders. On November 1st, you would move the November folder to the front of the numbers and place the October folder behind the numbered folders with the other months.

Correspondence Files

Instead of filing every piece of correspondence, which would only have to be eventually thrown away, create a correspondence notebook. Punch holes and put it in three ring binders. Or create a computer folder for correspondence.

Section Three

Time Saving Tools

Time Saving Tools

Computer

A computer is an absolute necessity. Internet access is a plus as you can connect with other resources in cyberspace. You should have financial software such as QuickBooks. (Web site-www.intuit.com) You will also need a word processing program such as Word Perfect or Word. If you make corporate presentations Power Point or Microsoft Publisher are terrific programs.

E-mail

No matter what kind of business. E-mail is a time saver. You can return messages at your convenience. Consumers also tend to be brief when writing e-mail.

Web Site

Besides adding credibility to your company, a web site can be a real time saver. You can advertise your services. Best of you can create a frequently asked questions section which can be a major time saver because you can reduce telephone inquiries (not to mention the mental, emotional and physical energy it takes to answer the same questions over and over again). These days you do not need to know HTML to design your own web site. Internet providers, such as America Online, often provide free web sites.

Other free Web Site providers also include http://www.About.com, http://www.Yahoo.com, and http://www.Geocities.com.

Telephone Equipment

A telephone with a headset makes it easier to take calls and retrieve customer information. A cordless telephone is also a necessary investment because you may need to move a quiet place if too much household noise interferes with a business call.

Homes with small children, or noisy teenagers also need a mute button. You can press the mute button and listen to your customer and reprimand your children at the same time.

Caller identification, Call waiting and conference calling are also features a home business may consider. You can ready your response for an irate customer before you pick up your telephone.

Call waiting assures that clients always get through to you and may give the appearance your business is larger than it is. It can also encourage customers to get to the point quickly.

Conference calls are essential if you want to avoid long meetings or going from place-to-place to confer with other business colleagues.

Answering Machine/ Answering Service

Unless you are constantly taking orders, a telephone can be a major disruption to your business.

Get a good quality answering machine and leave a clear message indicating your office hours and the designated hours you will return telephone calls. Be certain your answering machine has the following capacities, ability to record time and day you received the call and the capacity to take a lot of messages.

Sometimes people do not want to talk to an impersonal machine. It then becomes necessary to get an answering service. They are actually more economical than most people realize. You can instruct the service to call you with emergencies only.

Calendar

Every home office should have a large calendar. Besides using the calendar to mark appointments and significant dates, it helps you anchor your time. This calendar should be posted in your office wall or your desk. You need to be able to refer to it quickly. The calendar will help keep your personal and business commitments in balance because you can list things like your son's birthday and special projects on it as well. The larger the calendar the better. Stationary stores or office supply stores stock these calendars,

Calculator

You will need this for speedy calculations. While your computer may have one you need to have one that is portable.

Section Four

Office Essentials

Office Essentials

Desk

If you are purchasing a new desk be sure it has compartments and shelf space for reference books and materials. Remember your desk is not a filing cabinet. Do not pile papers on your desk. Remember your desk is a workplace not a storage place. If you find your desk is constantly cluttered then re-think your filing system.

Clock

A clock should be displayed near your desk Of course, if you use a computer this does not apply because a computer has a clock on it a computer. Without a clock you can lose track of time.

Vertical Desk Filing System

You will need a vertical filing system on your desk for current projects, accessible databases, etc. The traditional in/ out trays take up valuable desk space and encourage paper piling.

There are many vertical filing systems available. You may even purchase vertical magazine holders for this purpose. This file should contain materials you refer to daily. Categorize these folders in such areas " Correspondence", "To Do", "Staff" "Follow-up" "Delegate", etc.

Baskets/ Trays

Baskets or trays may needed for current or special projects . They can easily be removed from your desk when the project is completed. These baskets or trays can be carried around from room to room with you. On a sunny day you may want to work on the deck. You need only pick up your special project basket. Consolidate materials into one neat file when the project is completed as not to over stuff files with such materials.

White Space on Desk

Every desk should have a large clear area. A large calendar may delineate this area for you. A clear area helps you to think clear and gives you space to work on projects. Do not underestimate the value of white space on your desk. A clear desk helps you to think clearly and to approach your tasks optimistically.

Vertical Pen & Pencil Holders

Pens and pencils should be on your desk not in your desk. The ink will remain fresh and filtered downward if they are placed upright. More importantly, they are immediately accessible.
An inexpensive way to do this is to use old drinking glasses. A small memo pad should be located right next to the pencils as well.

Telephone

If you are left- handed your telephone should be on your right so you can answer the telephone too. Likewise if you are right handed the reverse applies. You should not have to stretch or get up to pick up the telephone this causes back strain which will eventually adversely affect your health over time.

Furniture

If you work at the computer you definitely need a swivel chair with wheels. Doctors and physical therapists are treating a whole sleuth of new maladies related to poor body alignment when working for long periods at the computer or your desk. Be certain your body is in proper alignment when working at your desk. Make certain your feet comfortably touch the floor.

Your back should be straight and your knees should bend comfortably in a 90-degree angle. Your wrist should be able to comfortably rest on the keyboard. You should be at least 18 inches from your computer screen. These variables are changing so check with your local office furniture store, which generally stays up to code in these issues.

Reference Books

If your desk has the room or storage space these books should be there. Of course, if you rarely use them, place them on a bookshelf.

Section Five

Organize Your Time

Organize Your Time

Daily Scheduling

Goal setting is the key to productivity. You should already have a business plan and have developed professional goals for your business. Each day you should work on some aspect of your goals. Your day should be organized around business goals.

You should have monthly, weekly and daily planning time to organize your time. Fix personal time with family and friends into your schedule in addition to goal activities..

There are basically two ways to organize your time. The first is most applicable to entrepreneurs. I refer" to it as division time organization." List the different divisions of your business and/or personal life. Then list the things to be done under each category. You can easily analyze the divisions you are neglecting. This is vital for a new business. See Below.

Marketing
1. Research magazine readership
2. Bookmark Sites
3. Update marketing plan

Human Resources
1. Schedule assistants for May seminar
2. Write job descriptions for future positions

Administrative
1. Return telephone calls
2. Fill daily booklet orders
3. Order more envelopes
4. Renew NAPO membership

Planning
1. Outline new book
2. Schedule time with Jeremy

Family Manager
1. Cook dinner
2. Take out summer clothes
3. Update bill system

Home Educator
1. Review curriculum
2. Submit quarterly report
3. Order books

The other way to organize your day is rather traditional. You simply list everything you have to do, and categorize by matter of importance:

1. Must Do
2. Should do
3. Could do

Tackle the "must-do" items first; check off each item as you do it. Remember; as a result of your weekly planning some fixed personal activities should have already been plugged into your day. These items should always be "must-do" items.

Another key to daily planning is self-evaluation of your daily activities. This is necessary to monitor your progress. You may approach it two ways.

You may journal. You need to ask yourself two key questions. Did I accomplish all I needed to do today? and "what can I do differently to be more productive tomorrow?" The answers to these questions should be brief and should be written right in your planner book.

The other method you may use to measure effectiveness is numeric assessment. Simply attach a numerical value to the different divisions of my business. (See divisions above) Then, list those divisions in order of importance, and circle the number you feel best corresponds to my level of effectiveness. You can thus work on the weak areas in your business. Think of it as your own employee evaluation.

Planner / Organizer

Get a personal digital assistant. There is Palm Pilots made by 3-Com. Casino, and Handspring are also two popular brands as well. Sony is developing its version of the digital assistant. Digital Assistants can be used to storage computer information and even communicate with others on the web. Read Consumers Report to determine the best one for your business.

Check out http://www.palmpilot.com, and http://www.handspring.com and http://www.casio.com These are excellent tools to integrate your home and business life together. You can have your shopping list in the same place you have your business contacts.

Section Six

Home
Business Distractions

Home Business Distractions

Interruptions

Do not engage in long conversations with people who interrupt you during business hours.

Post a "Do not disturb" sign on the door.

Arrange to have talkative customers or delivery people drop off materials when you are not home.

Speak to family members and friends tell them your goals. Let them know you will not be available during business hours.

Use your answering machine. Do not take personal calls during business hours.

Schedule time with family and friends so they will not interrupt office hours.

Temptations

Junk food-
Purchase only healthy food. Put break time in your regular schedule. Plan your meals. If you are hungry and meals are not planned the temptation is to grab a cookie or donut.

Make healthy food easily accessible. Fill a large drinking cup with water. Cut up fresh fruits and vegetables. Place them on the kitchen counter.

Television
Unplug the television. Turn on the radio for news. Check out the Internet new channels.

Daydreaming

Whenever you find yourself day dreaming, jot down a dot on an index card. Force yourself to get back to work. Set a goal for yourself to daily reduce the number of dots recorded.

Doing household tasks instead of business work

Organize your household. My book "Organize Your Home is a good place to start. Get household help if necessary. You need a clear clean environment to think clearly. The atmosphere of your home will affect your productivity. Don't ignore it. Be proactive about clearing it up.

Children in the home

Involve them in the business if you can. Teach them to file, fill orders, sort mail, and respond to e-mail. Be certain they use the spell checker. Children's wages are legitimate Internal Revenue deductions when they actually are working. It is a great experience for them as well. It is a win-win situation.

Little children can lick stamps, sort inventory, empty the wastebasket or dust the office. You can also get toddlers their own toy computer to play with while you are in the office. You may share childcare responsibilities with other parents. Or have a teenager care for your small children while you work. .

Most importantly, schedule time with your children so they do feel the business is more important than they are. It is easy for them to feel this way when all your mental and emotional energy goes into pleasing your customers and making money.

It is the little things we do everyday that help us to accomplish the big things!

Section Seven

Home Office Efficiency Tips

1. Set up accurate filing system so files do not pile on your desk.

2. Set up separate mail system. Mail system should be separate from your files.

3. Use a tickler file system if you have to keep appointment or frequently work away from your home.

4. Photocopy Schedule C (Internal Revenue Form for Small Business). Use the categories on Schedule C to make up a tax file.

5. Handle every piece of paper only once,

6. Schedule time in your day to open mail and to respond to the to-do items on your mail folder.

7. Use a calendar to post bills to give you a broad perspective of your finances.

8. Use technology. Buy a palm pilot or personal organizer. Sync information to your computer.

9. Visit Home Office web sites for ideas.

10. Keep a telephone log near telephone. Jot down information about telephone call and timing of incoming and outgoing calls. You will impress your clients.

11. When planning your day consider the personal and professional aspects of it. It is almost impossible to eliminate the personal aspects of working at home.

12. Occasionally take a day off. Don't go near the office (or the home office room or area)

13. Make certain there is white space or clear space on your desk. It helps you to think clear.

14. Play baroque music in your home office. This type of music will help you concentrate.

15. Occasionally get up from your desk stand tall and take a few deep breaths and stretch. It will revive you. You will find you can think clearer.

16. Put as much information as possible in electronic files on the computer. Information can be retrieved much easier and minimizes clutter.

17. Clean your house after work hours. A messy house can be distracting and thwart your productivity.

18. Get rid of your telephone books. The telephone book is on-line. Check out http://www.yellowonline.com

19. Invest in business books. Knowledge is power.

20. Subscribe to business e-zines (electronic magazines) instead of magazines. Less clutter and information is easily accessible.

21. Put reading time into your daily schedule. Professional journals are particularly important to the at-home worker because you need to stay abreast of industry trends.

22. Keep a marketing file of potential leads and new business opportunities.

23. Categorize your business books by subject or alphabetize them so you can easily locate them.

24. Invest in proper writing books for writing memos. Purchase a good dictionary, thesaurus.

25. Be certain to always use the spell check on your computer but don't rely solely on it.

26. Journal about your productivity at the end of the day. Analyze what works and what didn't work that day. Change accordingly.

27. Choose a location you will work comfortably in.

28. Invest in a telephone with a head set. You can move around and talk and dart into another room that is quiet.

29. If you have small children have a box of toys they can play with quietly when a client calls.

30. Clean your work area before you close your home office for the day. In fact consider ending the business day twenty minutes early just so you can clean and de-clutter office.

31. Paste business cards you receive right onto your roller decks.

32. Write personal information you want to remember about clients on the back of the card. Your clients will like your personal touch and you'll get plenty of referrals. People refer friendly people.

33. Schedule an out of the office lunch and breaks just as you would if you were in an office.

34. Make certain a large clock is in your view so you don't lose track of the time because other people are not around you.

35. Estimate the time it will take you to complete projects when you do your daily "to-do" list. (For example return telephone calls-estimated time- 45 minutes)

36. Wire your house with multiple telephone lines or use a cordless telephone so you can still pick up on business calls no matter where you are in the house.

37. Get a toll free number. They are quite inexpensive and give the appearance you are bigger than you really are. The added benefit is when you move your business number remains the same.

38. Exercise when you are feeling tired. It will revive you. The extra adrenaline will get the creative juices flowing. A real added advantage of being home. Can you imagine doing jumping jacks in the middle of the office?

39. Put time in your schedule for planning and organizing. Remember planning is setting goals and assessing your business mission. Organizing is making certain your plans can be carried out.

40. Schedule meetings with family members so they can know when you will be available to spend time with them.

41. Create a client profile. List client name, problem you solved and any pertinent personal information.

Put it in your files. Surprise them with a birthday call or a follow-up call.

42. Keep a personal file on your employees.

43. Make up a weekly "to-do" list for employees. Give it to them,

44. Schedule time to meet with employees weekly to assess their productivity.

45. Keep desk files vertical instead of horizontal. You have more desk space and you are more apt to file instead of pile.

46. Mount filing systems on the wall, to free up desk space.

47. Do your filing tasks daily.

48. When you take out a file put a piece of colored cardboard in the cabinet where the file was removed from so you can easily re-file it.

49. Invest in a laptop not a personal computer if you generally meet with clients outside your home office.

50. Make a financial plan for your business.

51. Decide in advance how the profits from the business should be used. Hint: they should be invested back in the business.

52. Check out used office supply stores for desks, chairs, tables, and filing cabinets –an economical way to

furnish your home office. Look them up in your local directory.

53. Join professional organizations of your trade (Accounting, Medical Record, Writing, etc.) and get involved in local chapters.

54. Schedule fun time with family and friends so they will know you care about them and you won't be emotionally tugged.

55. Purge your files regularly.

56. Use the mute button on your telephone when listening to a client and instructing the children to be quiet.

57. Put inspirational sayings and bible verses on your walls to encourage you.

58. Devise weekly goals for your business.

59. At the close of each day write your to-do list for the following day.

60. Give your children jobs in your business. Even small children can be a legitimate tax deduction if they engage in real work.

61. Donate your used equipment (Computer, fax, telephone, etc.) to charity when you upgrade. You will feel good and get a nice tax deduction.

62. Plan times of visiting others in similar businesses to discuss and network on business growth issues.

63. Get a good quality answering machine. Make certain your greeting sounds professional with no home noise in the background.

64. Don't take "personal" telephone calls during prescribed work hours.

65. Have calls forwarded to your cellular telephone or answering service if you work away from home a lot. People will feel better knowing they reach an actual person.

66. If you don't have space for an office, make a portable office out of a plastic storage container. Put files, info etc. in it.

67. Don't neglect your household tasks. Be certain to keep up with maintaining an orderly household.

68. Read books and newsletters on business growth.

69. Get audio books on Business growth.

70. Write a business plans for 5, 10,15 and even 20 years. Your priorities will change and you can chart your business growth based on those changing priorities.

71. Get help when you need it from accountants, professional organizers, artists, designers, etc. You cannot do it all by yourself. Know when you need help.

72. Dress for success. While you may enjoy the freedom of wearing your bathrobe often our clothing helps determine our attitudes. If we dress too laid back then we approach our work in a laid back fashion.

73. Take a speed reading class. Check your Continuing Education Division or local college.

74. Take a rapid writing/ speed writing class to increase your ability to take notes quickly while a client is talking.

75. File items vertically not horizontally in your desk draw.

76. Put desk organizers inside your desk draw to keep it organized.

77. Learn when to say "no". Don't just do something because someone asks you. Some distractions mask as business opportunities.

78. Make unimportant decisions quickly. The color of your printer paper will not make or break the business.

79. Have a designated time to return all business call. Afternoons are generally best to catch people in the office.

80. Create folders for your Internet mail and favorite sites.

81. Purchase a planner organizer.

82. Buy office supplies on-line. Most office supply stores have free delivery. Check to see if a store is in your area (See appendix for web sites and telephone numbers -Staples, Office Max, Office Depot etc.)

83. Keep a master list of office supplies so you can replenish your supply before you completely run out of anything.

84. Plan your meal times. Decide before hand what you will eat. Plan to eat healthy meals.

85. Organize your desk periodically during the day instead of waiting to the end of the day.

86. When cleaning off a sloppy desk put papers in broad categories then make sub-categories from those categories.

87. Set up a good filing system when you first set up your home office.

88. Separate your e-mail addresses into categories of clients and business people.

89. Attend industry conferences.

90. Write personal goals for yourself. If you pour all your energy into the business your personal life will suffer.

91. Find someone who is working at home like you to be accountable to in regards to your personal and business goals.

92. Post an encouraging saying on your computer screen saver.

93. Design how you would structure a perfect day using time slots.

94. Decide what you need to do reach your goal of a perfect day. After you determine what an ideal day would be, then make changes in your schedule to make it happen.

95. Ask yourself daily" how can I do this "better" Answers come to those who ask questions.

96. Use electronic assistants when possible. There are now web sites that will handle bookkeeping, bill payment, collection and even shopping for groceries.

97. Put pictures of kids on your desk as reminders of why you're working at home.

98. Do your business banking on-line or at 9 A.M.- 11 AM when banks are less crowded.

99. Open your mail near the wastebasket. Dump junk mail immediately.

100. Don't pick up mail until you are scheduled to open mail.

101. Purchase 'thank you" cards in bulk from an Office Supply store.

102. When a new issue of a magazine arrives throw away the old issue.

103. Get a big calendar that you can mark up and get rid of unnecessary paper.

104. Pre-pack your briefcase with a business book and audio cassette players with a good business tape so that you are always ready.

105. Establish definite hours to work in the business. You can even sign in and out if you tend to be a workaholic

106. Post a "do not disturb" sign on the door of your home office as a cue to family members you have put on your business hat.

107. If your home is messy, offer to pick up or delivery services for your customers.

108. Post business goals on the wall or put them in your electronic planner/organizer.

109. Don't turn on the television news. Listen to the radio instead.

110. If you are in a rut, get up walk around. Change something in your environment. You have the freedom to do that in your home office.

111. Occasionally leave your office. Work at the dining room table. Sometimes we need a change.

112. Use positive affirmations with yourself. I can do anything. I am empowered to succeed in all I do today.

113. Reward yourself for a job well done. Be careful with the calories.

114. Set deadlines. It will force you to work towards a goal.

115. Keep interruptions to a minimal. Don't talk to others during work time.

116.   Refuse to take personal telephone calls during business hours.

117.   Design a structured schedule with enough room for flexibility.

118.   Guard against daydreaming. Keep paper on your desk. Each time you find yourself daydreaming put a dot on the paper. Force yourself to get back to the work at hand. Keep pushing yourself to get fewer dots each day.

119.   Take frequent breaks so you do not get so drained or tire quickly.

120.   Set up files so you can easily retrieve customer information, names, dates, inventory and financial information.

121.   Do two things at once. Make dinner and check inventory.

122.   Keep a running list of things you can do in 5 minutes. When you are on hold do one of those things.

123.   Use postcards or e-mail to respond to customers' requests and questions.

124.   Create a customized form for common customer problems. (i.e.- In regard to your inquiry ABC Company will be sending out summer schedules to address the low inventory problem).

125.   Do personal and business errands at the same time.

126. Break large projects into smaller manageable parts.

127. Make temporary files relating to projects. When projects are completed, condense information into one small folder.

128. Keep a record of step by step process on how you completed a project.

129. Eliminate procrastination by breaking down overwhelming tasks into small steps.

130. Reward yourself after accomplishing even small tasks.

131. Create a beginning day ritual like completing a cup of coffee and an end day ritual like turning off the computer.

132. Schedule a day of leisure time regularly.

133. Plug non-work family items into your schedule far in advance of scheduled time. Never allow business to interfere with t these times.

134. Decide what success is for you. Home workers can be very driven.

135. Make realistic goals and enjoy completing them before you make new goals.

136. Contact SCORE (Service Corp of Retired Business Executives) for free business advice.

137. Set non-negotiable start/ end times for business meetings.

138. Keep your work area separate from the rest of the house.

139. Develop self-discipline. Read books on discipline.

140. Purge your business files regularly.

141. Unplug the television so it will not be a temptation for you.

142. Schedule free time for yourself.

143. Schedule appointments with clients before or after rush hours.

144. Hire a house cleaning service.

145. Place computer and technology receipts warranties and instruction books in one file.

146. Tape customer service telephone numbers for computer, fax, printer, copier, etc right inside desk draw or in vertical file on the desk. When a malfunction occurs you can quickly telephone for assistance.

147. Purchase a roll of stamps when you go to the Post Office instead of buying a few.

148. Order stamps through the mail. Pick up order form at the Post Office.

149. Once you pay a bill immediately file it.

150. Schedule one time a week to pay all your bills instead of doing it daily.

151. Schedule days or blocks of time when you will specifically work on marketing, finances, planning, organizing etc.

152. Use an egg or electric timer to make certain you maintain the time you have allotted to specific activities.

153. Use hanging files in your file cabinets.

154. Use transparent shoeboxes to store your office supplies.

155. Place papers in your file cabinet immediately. Never pile them on your desk.

156. Use caller identification to prepare yourself for customers' call.

157. Smile before you pick up the telephone. Even though your customer cannot see you your voice will sound more pleasant.

158. Summarize phone conversations so you can get off the telephone quickly. (i.e. Since we've discussed the meeting date, location and agenda let's just speak again on ....)

159. Put your office hours or the exact time you will receive telephone calls on your answering machine.

160. Carry a notebook around with you to jot down ideas that will grow your business.

161. Schedule daily quiet or thinking time. Do not just jump right into work.

162. Use a bank Christmas club to save money for your business.

163. Multi-colored milk crates are a great for files when there is no space for file cabinets.

164. Invest in comfortable chair if you are sitting most of the day.

165. Use self-stick stickers to make short personal notes to yourself.

166. Back up all information on computer disks

167. Compress your computer files frequently.

168. Utilize folders to organize business information in word processing or web programs.

169. Make an appointment with yourself daily to brainstorm new ideas for your business.

170. Consolidate similar business and home activities together. Pay your business bills and personal bills if you have your banking statement and financial records out.

171. Carry your planner/organizer at all times.

172. Call to confirm all appointments.

173. Listen to a self-improvement tape while cleaning or traveling.

174. Make certain the items on your desk are accessible to you easily. You should be able to answer the telephone while still typing.

175. Put reference materials within arm's reach.

176. Get off junk mailing list. Contact Mail Preference of the Direct Marketing Association, 11 West 42nd Street, PO 3861, New York, New York 10163-3861

177. Create an inactive file box for old tax and business records.

178. Put preparation time in your schedule.

179. Do not send an unsolicited fax.

180. Don't put your fax number on your business card it encourages junk fax. (or enlarge your business number so the fax is not readily noticeable)

181. Make certain your fax has enough memory in case you run out of paper.

182. When calling someone else always state the exact purpose of your call and the exact time you will be available for the call to be returned.

183. Divide desk drawers into four quadrants and clean out a section at a time.

184. Divide a messy desk into quadrants and deal with the mess in small increments.

185. If you are right-handed put your telephone on the left so you can take notes with your right hand.(and vice versa,).

186. When removing papers from a messy desk put papers in high priority A (paper requiring action) , and low priority (papers requiring filing) so you can still keep your business running.

187. Delegate as much as possible to others.

188. Ask for help. Even your neighbor can assist you.

189. Cut articles you want to read out of journals. Paste them to 8 x 11 paper and put in three ring binders.

190. Learn to skim articles to determine if you want to read the whole article.

191. Get business books reviews: you don't have to read the whole book.

192. Simplify your home office.

193. De-clutter your home. Cut down on dusting and cleaning.

194. Organize your home,

195. Schedule less demanding tasks when your energy level is low-like late afternoon.

196. Make an appointment with your secretary or assistant regularly.

197. Get Quicken accounting for organizing financial records.

198. Mount a wipe board on the wall.

199. Remove all paper clips before filing papers.

200. Don't overstuff files.

201. Throw out old out-dated or duplicate information when filing a new document.

202. Label all folders in capital letters.

203. Never let file grow thicker than bigger than ¾ of an inch.

204. Make a filing master sheet listing all your files.

205. Punch holes in newsletters and store them in three ring binders.

206. Review files. If you haven't used a file in a year move it to your inactive file box.

207. Keep tax records for at least seven years after you have filed your return.

208. Date papers before they are filed

209. Practice relaxation techniques. Deep breathing or visualizing peaceful place.

210. Type your document in your word processing program and format it after it is completely typed.

211. Label and date all your file storage boxes.

212. Plan both snacks and meals.

213. Be creative with your schedule. You do not have to keep typical office hours. The sky's the limit when you work at home.

214. Have talkative clients or delivery people drop off material when you are not home.

215. Get your own web site. Make a Frequently Asked Questions section to reduce telephone inquiries.

217. Contact your local university to get a college intern.

216. Design a marketing plan. Work on marketing aspects daily.

216. Write a price list for your services. You should not agonize each time you get an inquiry.

217. Take your business cards with you when you go on personal errands. Let others know what you are doing.

218. Hire welfare clients to help with your business. Besides getting the help you need your altruism will give big tax breaks. Call 1-800-872-5621 or visit www.welfaretowork.org.

219. Pre-select two or three business outfits (complete with accessories) you will wear when you do business outside the office.

220. Instead of stewing over issues, write a letter to the editor and get the added bonus of free publicity.

221. Try the free web electronic organizer . Go to http://www.eorganizer.com

222. Use the United States Postage priority mail envelopes. It will save you time and money.

223. The United States Postal Service offers a free seminar "Making Direct Mail Easy" Seminars. Visit web site http://usp.com or check with your local post office for more information.

224. Have a business lunch in your home.

225. Have a positive attitude and be pleasant with your customers. Your business will grow as a result of referrals and you will enjoy it more yourself.

226. Subscribe to web newspapers instead of cluttering your office with daily newspapers.

227. Bank on-line.

228. Create an advisory council utilizing friends and family. Present your problems to them and let them spend time brainstorming business solutions.

229. Hire a Professional Organizer.

230. Put your computer, fax, etc on a maintenance schedule.

231. Carry a tape recorder with you especially when you get a thought when you are driving.

232. Make time to train your children and others that can assist you in business. Do not just assign a task

to them Make certain they fully understand what is expected of them.

233. Take time midday to stop pray or reflect.

234. Make an appointment quarterly to spend the entire day organizing and de-cluttering your home office extensively.

235. Get an accountability partner who is in a similar business.

236. Stock up on office supplies in September when you can catch back-to-school sales.

237. Listen to self-improvement tapes weekly.

238. Put something on your desk to make you smile: a child's drawing or a silly saying, etc.

239. Put upbeat music on when you want to move faster.

240. Plan your schedule loosely with room for surprises.

241. Remove outdated file when you file new documents.

242. Get enough sleep.

243. Reduce visual clutter. Your desk and office surfaces should be clear.

244. Write a structured daily schedule. Post the schedule in your home office and on your refrigerator. Others will know your schedule.

245. Ask other family members about their goals and share yours with them too.

246. Write a company mission statement that inspires you.

247. Learn to say "no" without guilt.

248. Work at low concentration tasks when you are doing a household task. You can think of ideas for an article while folding the laundry.

249. Make a master list of all the contents of your inactive files and where you have stored them.

250. Contact your local elected officials ask them to keep you abreast of the changing home office deduction.

251. Take time when you first enter your office in the morning to make sure the office is in order.

252. Take credit cards. Your business will increase substantially with the same efforts.

253. Give attention to small children before you make a block of telephone calls.

254. Barter services with other business people.

255. Invest in comfortable office furniture so that you will want to stay at your desk longer.

256. Color code files based on clients or business categories.

257. Invest in lateral filing cabinet instead of standard household file cabinet. Check out used office furniture stores.

258. Encourage employee accountability by assigning a user code to employees for fax, copier, and telephone use.

259. Purchase large carbon copy receipt book so both you and your customers have a record of transactions. You can also enclose these copies when you mail standard bills even though these receipts will be discarded on the other end. You will still have a hardcopy record of all financial transactions.

260. For more organizing ideas visit http://napo.net

261. Put ordering new organization products in your schedule regularly.

262. Hang a small bulletin board on the wall for little notes to yourself and inspirational quotes.

263. Set a deadline for all tasks.

264. Share your deadline with others.

265. Do the unpleasant tasks first. Harness ability to complete a task by visualizing the end.

266. Form positive habits. Write down which habits you need to develop.

267. Play "beat the clock" with yourself. (Use a timer.)

268. Work in shifts. You mat work three hours in the morning. Take two hours to clean the house and make dinner, then return to the office for another three hours. Plan your schedule accordingly.

269. Do not over-commit. You cannot be at the scouting meeting and the blood drive at the same time.

270. Make certain all your goals are specific.

271. Do not be a perfectionist about your business tasks.

272. Visualize the task completed.

273. Buy home office supplies on-line. (See appendix F)

274. Set a stop watch to ring at a specified time when working with talkative clients. You can then inform the client who also hears the alarm that you have something you need to do now.

275. Check out Quickbooks Intuit for bookkeeping.

If you want to know, you must first ask. Answers come to those courageous enough to ask.

Cleaning Your desk

- How to get rid of all the clutter - and piles of files - on your desk.

- How to create and use your Master List.

- How to make your desk work for you.

- How to create and use your Master File system.

- How to organize your Master File drawer.

- How to organize the drawers in your desk.

and more

<u>Section Eight</u>

Frequently Asked Questions

Question
Can you tell me what file categories I should have?

Answer
No. Look at your business papers. What are your broad categories?. Every business has fiscal files but a service orientated business runs very differently than a business with inventory. You can talk with other entrepreneurs in your field to determine your exact file names. Your business plan should also direct you as to the file categories you need.

Question
I have my home office in an excellent place but I'm not as productive as I want to be. What can I do?

Answer
The number one rule in home office productivity is location, location, and location. You will only work in your office if you are comfortable. Some home workers make their office in their closets then wonder why they are not productive. A closet can be very claustrophobia. A kitchen table might be a more productive place., although of course it won't be as quiet. A practical solution may be to put your files in the closet but to work at your kitchen table.

Question
What if I have no place for a home office?

Answer
You can create a portable office by putting business items in a 20-gallon plastic storage bin, or a lager one. (From a Kmart, Wal-Mart, Kohl's, Sears, etc.) You can purchase file boxes for your files. You can stack them in a corner or conceal them in your closet.

Question

My business work spills into every room of the house. What can I do?

Answer

Perhaps your home office is not in a place that encourages you to work at your desk. Re-locate your office to another part of the home. If this is not possible re-design your home office so it is more pleasant. Add plants, comfortable chairs, family pictures, and inspirational plaques.

Also, sometimes when business spills into every room it is an indication of faulty scheduling. Are you trying to keep up with household tasks and business tasks at the same time? This is not necessarily a bad thing but if you are not being productive in either your home or business then you need to take a long at your schedule. You will have to scale back in business or home duties.

Question

My home is a mess. I find it difficult to just go to my home office when my house is in such a mess. So every morning I get started late because I am doing something in the house. What should I do?

Answer

Your home office is affected by your home. Take the time to put your home in order. Read my book' Organize Your Home!

Question

I work harder at home than I ever did at the office. I know I should be keeping my home office in order but at the end of the day I am just so tired. What can I do?

Answer

You need to put organizing your home office in order. Schedule breaks. Take time to stand stretch or do light aerobic exercise. You will have more energy to get more done. Be certain also that you do not over-schedule. Home workers also tend not to ask for help. If keeping the books overwhelm you, then hire a bookkeeper or an accountant. You do not have to do it all! Likewise you may need to hire household help at times. Do not hesitate to ask for help when you find yourself buried in your work.

Question

What is a master filing sheet and why do I need it?

Answer

A master-filing sheet is where you write down the names of all of your files. You can easily locate what category you filed something under. You will feel more confident about filing your papers. Often people have cluttered desk because they are afraid they will not be able to find an important document. You will be more apt to file a paper if you can recall where it is filed immediately.

Question

How can I get more desk space?

Answer

Mount as many things on the wall. Or get a desk hutch it mounts right on top of your desk.

Question

I keep getting interrupted by everyone. I can't get anything done. What can I do?

Answer

You have to set the barometers. Don't stop to talk long to anyone who interrupts your work schedule. When you talk you condition people to repeat the same behavior. Post a "do not disturb" sign and enforce the law..

Question

How can I keep better tax records?

Answer

Photocopy Internal Revenue Service Schedule C, (Deductions for small business). Label your files according to the categories they have listed. At the end of the tax year total the deductions then place these tax files in your inactive file storage box. Then create new files for the current tax year.

Question

How does having a business plan help me to be more productive?

Answer

Because you become goal driven. Goals drive you. Without a business plan everything will look like a good opportunity when in reality nit might merely be a distraction.

Questions

I'm buried under paperwork. Where do I start?

Answer

Set up your filing system first. You may have to take an entire business day to put your filing system in order. When you begin to remove papers from your desk be certain you put them in categories high priority to low priority. The high priority items you need to act on to keep the business running smoothly. Current projects, for example, should not be piled up with old documents. Low priority things need to be filed. If you are in a big heap of papers that is hindering your business then you may need to get a Professional Organizer who specializes in home offices or paper management. Visit http://organizerswebring.com Or visit http://www.napo.net

Question
Isn't it my secretary's responsibility to keep the office in order?

Answer
It is her responsibility to assist you in your business. She can be a greater help to you if both of you work at keeping the office in order.

Question
I work hard all day but I can't see why all my time is going?

Answer
Do an inventory of your time to determine what you are doing. Record what you are doing in increments of fifteen minutes for two days. Analyze your activities. Disorganization robs most people of their productivity.

Question
Do you advocate having a separate business and personal organizers?

Answer
People should plan and organize their personal and business lives. Each one affects the other. You should have one that addresses the needs of both your personal and business life. Digital organizing

assistants now make it possible to accomplish this easily.

Question
If I have a Palm Pilot, why do I need a large calendar in my home office?

Answer
You need to visually see your work commitments in their totality. It aids you in seeing the big picture in regards to deadlines, family commitments, etc.

Question
You advocate employing your children to get them to help out in my business so they can feel more a part of it. Each time my children help they make more work for me. Any ideas?

Answer
You need to take the time to train your children before you assign them a task. Train them long before you need their help, perhaps in non-business hours. First, invite them to observe you engaged in the task you that want to assign them. Next let them help you in the task. Next supervise them while they do the task. Finally assign them the task when they no longer need your supervision.

Question
Are mail folders part of my filing system?

Answer
No, unless you are involved in the mail order business where your mail is your business. Your filing system should be totally separate from your mail system.

Question

I work with disorganized clients. They lose all my correspondence, fail to return calls and are always late. What can I do?

Answer

You cannot do much to change someone else. You can keep a telephone log of conversations, send reminder notices and follow-up post cards. Always call to confirm meetings. Document your interactions with them and anticipate they will not be timely and plan accordingly.

Question

I don't know what kind of home business I want to start yet but I do know I need to be organized first. I am terribly disorganized. All the books I read say I should be organized, where should I start?

Answer

Organize your personal life and your home first. This is most important organize yourself first. Create a business plan to determine your professional goals. Next set up your filing s or inventory system. Set up your desk making certain there is abundant white space (clear space). Do a lot of reading and contact a professional or trade association.

Question

How do I know what files to throw away?

Answer

You need to hold on to tax papers for at least seven years. Generally you can file questionable papers in the inactive file box. Date the box. If you do not refer to the contents for at least a year (longer for legal and personal records) then you can discard the whole box.

Question

I home-school and work at home. My office is always in a mess and I often struggle with my business and family time. Where can I start?

Answer

First give serious time to planning for your home-schooling your children first. Once your home-schooling goals are clear then proceed with business planning.

Once you make plans, then you can organize your time in your home business and children's' education. I also offer these practical tips: maintain a home-school plan book, a daily business plan book.

Prioritize your education and business activities. Get help with household tasks, accounting, or legal matters. You may be doing too much. Be flexible in scheduling time. Above all make certain you have time for yourself. I know this is difficult but you need time to look at the big picture in business and your home-schooling endeavors.

Question

How do I know when my home office has outgrown my home, or am I just sorely disorganized?

Answer

That's a personal question. If you want to move out of your home, then that is when your revenue can sustain it. If you do not want to move out your home then I suggest organizing your space or re-locating your office in another part of the house. Once you have exhausted all organizing possibilities in your home then its time for you to move.

Question
What is baroque music and how does it help me work better?

Answer
Baroque music is a type of classical music with helps you to relax and thus concentrate more. Check it out in your local music store or try a musical on-line store.

Appendix A

Office Supply stores

Staples
http://www.staples.com

Office Max
http://www.officemax.com

Office Depot
http://www.officedepot.com

Viking Office Supplies
http://www.vikingop.com

Quill Products
http://www.quillcorp.com

Appendix B

Web sites of interest to at- home businesses

Information for the at home worker
http://www.workingsolo.com

Information for women entrepreneurs
http://onlinewbc.org

Information for Mothers working at Home
http://www.mhbn.com
http://www.bizymom.com

General Small Business Information
http://www.bizoffice.com
http://www.businessknowhow.com

United States Small Business Administration
http://www.sba.gov

United States Post Office
http://www.usps.com

Appendix C

Toll Free Numbers. Get one for your business.

MCI Worldcom 1-800-888-0800

US Sprint 1-800-877-2000

AT&T 1-800-222-0400

Internet Search 1-800 numbers

SCORE
Service Corp of Retired Executives offers free business counseling for small business. Write to SCORE, Evergreen Commons, 480 State Street, Holland, MI 49423. Web Site- http://www.score.org

Eorganizer.com
Free Internet Organizer.
http://eorganizer.com

Appendix D

Time Chart. Please record an average day in increments of fifteen minutes

Time	Activity	Time	Activity

Appendix E

Make goals in the different areas of your life

Personal Goal Sheet

Post it where you can see it daily!

Personal Mission Statement:

Long term Goals (with deadlines):

Financial:

Physical:

Mental:

Family:

Professional:

Social:

Spiritual:

Business:

Appendix F

Organizing Products

QuickBooks Intuit, Inc.
PO Box 7850
Mountain Valley CA 94039-7850
http://www.intuit.com
800-433-8810,

Home Office Materials
Organization Etc.
3036 S. Fremont Avenue
417-882-3336
http://www.org-etc.com

Get Organized!
600 Cedar Hollow Road
Paoli, PA 19301
Fax-610-725-1144
http://www.getorginc.com

Stacks & Stacks
http://www.stacksandstacks.com
Toll free number-1-877-278-2257

Organize-It
133 S. Livernois
Rochester Hills, MI 48307
Toll Free number -1-800-210-7712

Lillian Vernon
Lillian Vernon Corporation
Virginia Beach, Virginia 23479
Toll free number- 1-800-LILLIAN (545-5426)
http://www.lillianvernon.com

Visit these web sites
www.organize123.org

www.add123.org

http://www.organizeyourworld.com

http://www.rubbermaid.com

http://www.eorganizer.com

http://www.napo.net

http://www.organizerswebring.com

About the Author

Cheryl R. Carter is a home based worker. She has worked with groups and individuals to increase personal productivity and organization.

Contact her at:

Jehonadah Communications
Post Office Box 712
Long Island, New York 11553-0712

E-mail-Cheryl@Organize123.org

www.ingramcontent.com/pod-product-compliance
Lightning Source LLC
Chambersburg PA
CBHW071254170526
45165CB00003B/1345